# ISABELLA BLOW

MARTINA RINK

# ISABELLA BLOW

IMAGES:

On the jacket: This portrait of Isabella Blow by Donald McPherson has never previously been published and has been residing in Donald's personal archives since it was taken in 2001. Donald and Isabella were lunching with the Al Sabah family (the Royal Family of Kuwait) at a desert party near the Kuwaiti border. Isabella is dressed in Alexander McQueen and is wearing a Philip Treacy hat.

Endpapers: Designed by Richard Woods. Famous for transforming environments and architecture, Woods' first printed floor commission was for Isabella and Detmar. He has since transformed the Comme de Garçons store in Osaka, Deitch projects and Modern Art gallery, London, and his work has been featured in the Venice Biennale.

Frontispiece: Isabella Blow, photographed by Phil Poynter

First published in the United Kingdom in 2010 by
Thames & Hudson Ltd, 181A High Holborn,
London WC1V 7QX
www.thamesandhudson.com

First published in 2010 in hardcover in the United States of America by
Thames & Hudson Inc., 500 Fifth Avenue, New York, New York 10110
thamesandhudsonusa.com

Compiled by Martina Rink with Natasha Isaacs
Produced and designed by Paul Sloman for Thames & Hudson
Assistant: Christine Antaya
With special thanks to Philip Treacy and Julia Delves Broughton

British Library Cataloguing-in-Publication Data
A catalogue record for this book is available from the British Library
Library of Congress Catalog Card Number 2010923361

ISBN: 978-0-500-51535-8

Printed and bound in Italy

# CONTENTS

FOREWORD BY

PHILIP TREACY

# FOREWORD

## BY PHILIP TREACY

In the past few years, Isabella Blow has been eulogized and analyzed by some of the world's most important fashion personalities, designers and journalists. A comment on the internet after one such article was: "Why is everybody writing and talking about this woman? She only wore funny hats and clothes."

To see Isabella in all her finery, two-dimensionally in a magazine or newspaper, was one experience; to meet her and interact with her was to witness another dimension entirely. Isabella walked to the beat of her own drum. Her personality, her intelligence and her magic far transcended any hat or dress she could have worn.

She single-handedly, and with impressive conviction, invented and defined the careers of the international fashion designer Alexander McQueen and a hat designer, me, the supermodel Stella Tennant and the model and author Sophie Dahl, amongst many others.

She nurtured and influenced the careers of many of today's most important fashion photographers, giving many of them their first break in an industry that is difficult to crack. She supported, promoted and enhanced the careers of some of today's most prolific contemporary artists.

Her fearlessness, in an industry that runs on fear, is legendary; she was a champion of young creative people without a voice. While she endeavoured to work within today's world of corporate fashion cannibalism, her ultimate ethos was a passionate belief that fashion is about a pursuit of beauty, elegance and creativity.

Isabella Blow with Philip Treacy, photographed by Kevin Davies
Courtesy Kevin Davies

LEFT TO RIGHT:

Philip and Isabella when they
first met, at her desk at *Tatler*

Isabella in Philip's shop at
69 Elizabeth Street,
working the telephone

Isabella in Philip's shop

Isabella upstairs at
67 Elizabeth Street

Isabella cooking in the
kitchen at 67 Elizabeth Street
when Philip first met her

Isabella before she left for
her father's funeral. She said:
"I don't have to look poor."

Isabella on her way out for the
evening with Detmar, having
collected a hat to wear from
Philip's studio

Philip would sometimes
polaroid Isabella in her hats
at his studio

Isabella in Philip's shop at
69 Elizabeth Street after work

Isabella in Philip's shop

Isabella at 67 Elizabeth Street
with smudged lipstick

Isabella in Philip's first studio
at 67 Elizabeth Street

# ISABELLA BLOW

## AN INTRODUCTION

**A**ttempting to capture the essence of Isabella Blow in a few words is a challenge even for those closest to her. A bit of Edith Sitwell, a touch of the Marchesa Casati; a cross between a Billingsgate fishwife and Lucretia Borgia; Marlene Dietrich and Leigh Bowery: the list of names recalled in an effort to describe her is as endless as it is unusual. Yet Isabella, to those who knew her either personally or even as the larger-than-life figure that took centre-stage on catwalk front rows, was beyond comparison.

Isabella was unique and had no predecessor. In a world where everyone chased the latest fashion designers, she set about discovering and creating them. From the moment she bought the entire degree show of Alexander McQueen in 1991 and called upon the student Philip Treacy to design hats for her wedding, she began a practice of nurturing new talents that would come to define her life in the fashion world. Rarely seen in public without a Treacy hat and matching designer outfit, her appearance was more than matched by her personality. An incredible ability to articulate her ideas in tantalising soundbites gave a frequent glimpse into the mind of a captivating woman who left an impression on everyone whose lives crossed with hers. As well as being one of fashion's great performers, her career was punctuated by jobs at *Vogue* and *Tatler*, and her desire to give a platform to emerging designers was only made possible by her own skills as a stylist for fashion shoots that captured the dark beauty of her own imagination.

\*

From the moment that Anna Wintour, editor-in-chief at American *Vogue*, gave Isabella her first major break in 1984, she instantly began to send reverberations throughout the creative community of New York. America and the world got its first introduction to the extraordinary and conflicted personality that was to become a permanent fixture in the fashion world for the next two decades. Her journey to *Vogue* had been a long one. Born Isabella Delves Broughton in 1958, she grew up with her sisters Julia and Lavinia, having

Isabella Blow, photographed
by Rankin
Courtesy Rankin

lost her brother at a young age. She was educated in the UK at Heathfield and had her first taste of New York in 1979 when she studied at Columbia University. Her first introduction to the fashion industry came in 1981, when Bryan Ferry introduced her to Anna. It was an introduction that she would remember, and she focused her attentions on developing it during her subsequent years in Texas, where she lived in an arid town, "the kind of place you drive through to get to somewhere else," with her first husband Nicolas Taylor.

Two years later, following some sleight-of-hand on her CV, Isabella persuaded Anna to take her on at *Vogue*. Keen to shake off the dust of her Texan existence, she set about making New York her home immediately, establishing a reputation within the city's artistic community and bringing it, in all its rawness, into the office of Condé Nast itself. Famously, it became common to find the artist Jean-Michel Basquiat at *Vogue*, waiting to share the company of Isabella. Pop artist Andy Warhol was another.

From those early days, the unique contrast of high fashion and chaotic discord that was to define her public persona was there in full force. "Once," Anna Wintour recalled in her memorial speech in 2007, "she wore an elaborate sari creation that unravelled as she exited the Condé Nast building on Madison Avenue. She didn't notice – or didn't care – and hopped into a cab, only to get the fabric caught in the door. The last anyone saw of Issy that day was the silk sari streaming in the tailwind, heading uptown." The relationship between Isabella and *Vogue* was more than just professional. In a letter to writer and artist Liza Campbell, Isabella said: "*Vogue* is like joining a church. It is a whole new perspective on life." And for *Vogue*, the presence of Isabella amongst its congregation was equally inspiring. In Wintour's words, "Dressing up was about making her job into an event. Issy had the most wonderful ability to elevate even the most basic of tasks and turn it into something memorably thrilling – to the extent that the task of cleaning her desk every night had to be done with a bottle of Perrier water and Chanel No. 5." By 1986, Isabella's baptism at Condé Nast had set her up for a career in fashion, and she moved back to the UK to take up a new post at *Tatler* in London. It was during this period that

she began to use her new-found influence to start nurturing those that inspired and influenced her.

*

Of those with whom she developed lifelong working and personal relationships, none came close to the one she developed with Philip Treacy. Born in County Galway, Philip studied fashion design at the National College of Art and Design in Dublin before moving to London to take up a place at the Royal College of Art. It was during his first year in 1989, when he was visiting the offices of *Tatler* to pick up a hat he had made for a photo shoot, that he was invited to meet someone known as "Issy." In came Isabella, "this very striking and slightly intimidating woman," in his own words. He "was completely blown away while she asked me some incredibly serious questions, and mentioned that she wore hats."

The next day, while he was at college, Isabella got in touch and put in an order for a series of hats for her forthcoming wedding to Detmar Blow. Philip, still a student and with no business to his name, found that Isabella was about to bring his career to life for the first time. As fashion editor at *Tatler*, she had the pick of famous designers across the world at her fingertips, but her decision to take on an untested student served as a reflection of what motivated her. While everyone else was looking to the catwalks for inspiration, she preferred to wear what she liked, and let the catwalks follow. Her unfailing eye for creative potential meant that her love of fashion went deeper than it did for many who circled the industry, and by daring to invest her faith in new avenues of creativity, she began to mould a corner of the fashion world in her own image.

The synergy between Philip and Isabella emerged from fashion, but while Philip's hats appeared primarily to function as objects of aesthetic beauty, she was often quick to give the relationship added depth. Of Isabella, Philip said: "I was so inspired by the way she wore my hats. She wore them like she was not wearing them – like they happened to be there." And of Philip, Isabella had much to say, too: "He's like a cosmetic surgeon for your face. Your face has a different personality for each one you're wearing."

The theatre and performance of fashion, and the way in which it disguised, dressed up and exploited different aspects of the personality that lay beneath the surface, went to the heart of the challenging image that Isabella represented. Often exploring the subject of her own appearance, she regularly expressed contradictory views, once describing her own face as "ugly. I know that's subjective, so perhaps I should stay instead that I'm striking. My face is like a Plantagenet portrait."

And indeed the hats she wore did go beyond normal expectations, bringing to life visions of extraordinary and unexpected detail, whether it was a jewel-encrusted lobster for Julien Macdonald's fashion show in 1998, or a Japanese garden complete with temples and trees for Alexander McQueen. But a Philip Treacy hat was not just to mask the face, or to turn it into something else. Isabella voiced more whimsical reasons to keep her head adorned: to prevent air-kissing amongst "all and sundry," and to provide something to be removed in the act of love-making. She also made other claims that deliberately called into question the world in which she operated, as well as the place she inhabited within it: "Fashion is a vampiric thing. It's the hoover on your brain. That's why I wear the hats, to keep everyone away from me."

\*

As Isabella flourished during the 1990s, her own unique vision of beauty and the world had its opportunity to bloom. And it was a vision that, more often than not, harnessed the beauty of medieval gothicism.

The fashion shows of Spring 1996 were particularly pregnant with Isabella's realisation of the erotic macabre. While the hats in Philip's collection included a pheasant perched on the head, a python that coiled around in implicit con-

2003, she organised a shoot for *Tatler* that would push the boundaries of seduction and verge on the instant gratification she had hinted at.

Art director Leon St Amour and photographer Robert Astley Sparke were accompanied by Isabella as she began to style a shoot that required all the models to pose with one breast exposed. She named it *Nipples in Naples*, an idea that superseded her original concept, *No Muff too Tough*, which *Tatler* had already decided was an idea too far. Isabella insisted that her assistant would also feature in the shoot, but she was nervous and reluctant; it was her first day. Astley Sparke, who was relatively new to the job, did not feel entirely comfortable either, and expressed apprehension about executing her orders. So to encourage the others, Isabella went first, posing stridently for a photograph that made the first double spread of the subsequent piece in *Tatler*.

But it was not all about titillation. Hats were littered liberally about the shoot, and the Italian setting had all the decadent grandeur that was her trademark. The photographs harnessed the damaged beauty of Naples' architecture, and added a dash of gaudy humour. The result was a news story in itself.

An Isabella Blow shoot was always an event. During the first Gulf War, photographer and long-time collaborator Donald McPherson seized a spontaneous opportunity to photograph her on the Kuwaiti border. The result, a vision of Isabella triumphantly dressed in Treacy mask and flying cape, captured the raw power that her image could conjure. In the later stages of her career, she flew out to New Delhi in a typically extreme one-person attempt to harness the potential of Indian fashion. Recalling the moment, Leon St Amour remembers being called up to fly out and join her. On arriving in his hotel room he turned on the television and there she was, taking over the news channels, declaring her mission to save the Indian fashion industry.

Such stories may illustrate that Isabella's performance may have been, as Anna Wintour has suggested, about "making her job into an event," but when she worked on shoots it was about much more. While styling for photographer and

# LETTERS TO

# ISABELLA BLOW

# JULIA DELVES BROUGHTON

## ISABELLA'S SISTER

Isabella lived life as a piece of theatre, a performance in which she insisted she took the lead role.

Her desire to take centre-stage began in childhood, when she competed single-mindedly for attention; it was a competitive instinct that took no prisoners, but it was also what contributed to her being such a unique character; so wonderfully warm, charming and generous.

Growing up with Isabella was incredibly exciting. Without her, life is like a stage without a star.

Julia, left, with Isabella, right, photographed by Lenare
Courtesy Julia Delves Broughton

# MARIO TESTINO

## PHOTOGRAPHER

MARIO TESTINO

BEING WITH HER MEANT THAT
ANYTHING COULD HAPPEN AT A SHOW,
A PARTY OR AN EVENT...

FEW PEOPLE TAKE IT TO THAT
LEVEL AS MOST PEOPLE JUST WANT TO FIT IN.

ISSY JUST DIDN'T CARE.
WE NEED ANOTHER ISSY.

*Mario*

FACING PAGE AND FOLLOWING SPREAD: Isabella Blow, photographed by Mario Testino
Courtesy Mario Testino

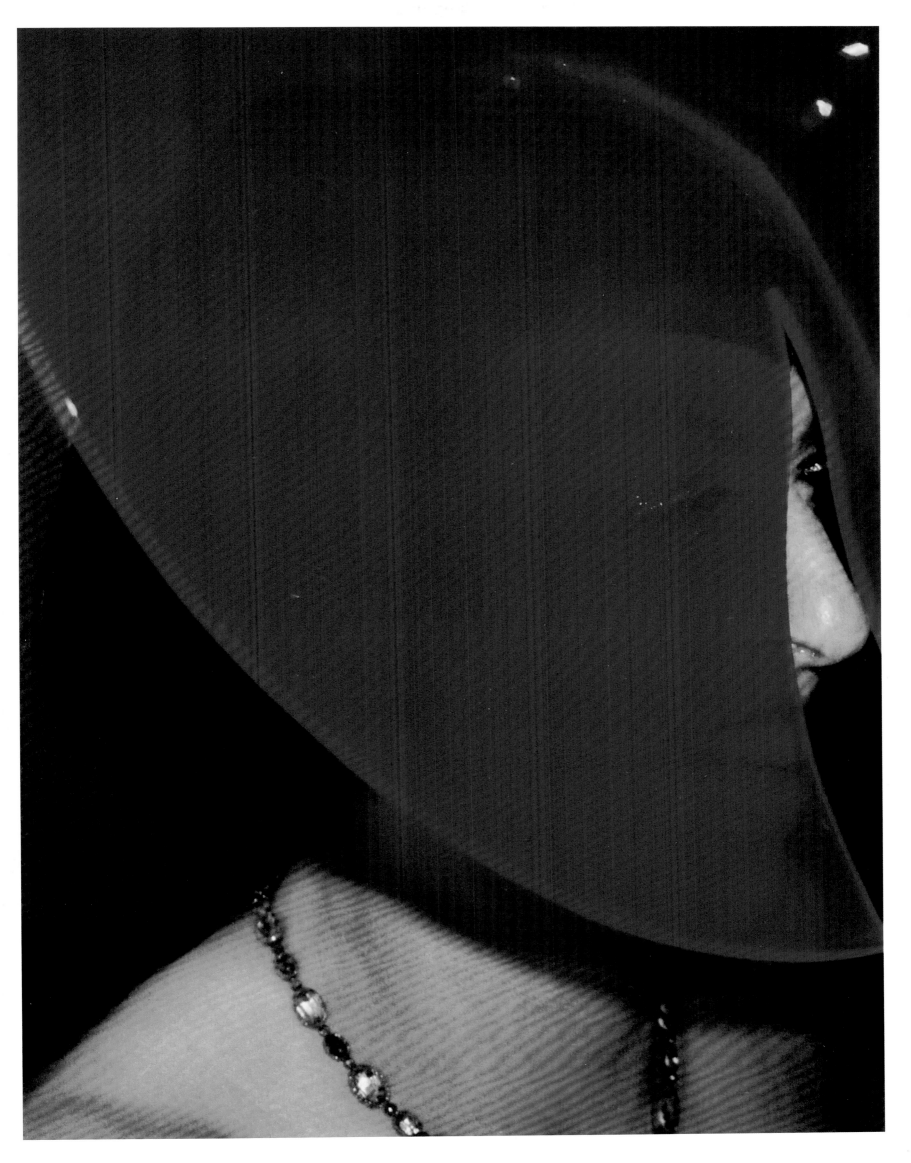

# RICHARD BURBRIDGE

## FASHION PHOTOGRAPHER

ISSY AGREED TO BE PHOTOGRAPHED BY ME FOR A STORY ON HER IN AMERICAN VOGUE.

I REMEMBER THE SHOOT VERY CLEARLY.

SHE NEVER SAT STILL FOR A SECOND, TALKED NON STOP, LAUGHED HER HEAD OFF AND RECALLED OVER AND OVER AGAIN THE TIMES WE HAD PREVIOUSLY SPENT TOGETHER. THE PICTURE THAT RAN REFLECTED THIS. (NOT THE IMAGE OPPOSITE)

ON SEEING IT IN THE MAGAZINE SHE CALLED MY STUDIO AND LEFT AN IMPASSIONED MESSAGE ON MY ANSWER MACHINE TELLING ME THAT IT WAS THE MOST DISGUSTING THING THAT SHE HAD EVER SEEN.

A FEW YEARS PASSED AND WHEN WE MET AGAIN SHE TOLD ME THAT I HAD MADE HER LOOK LIKE SHE WAS ABOUT TO SUCK MY COCK. TO MAKE MATTERS WORSE WE WERE SITTING IN A CROWD OF PEOPLE WHO WERE WATCHING HER AND LISTENING TO EVERY WORD.

HOWEVER THIS PHOTOGRAPH IS ONE THAT SHE LIKED AND WAS USED IN THE BOOK PHILIP TREACY, 'WHEN PHILIP MET ISABELLA'

WITH ISSY YOU NEVER KNEW QUITE WHAT TO EXPECT. SHE ALWAYS LOOKED FOR THE EXCEPTIONAL AND SHE TRULY WAS UNIQUE. I REALLY MISS HER A LOT.

Isabella Blow, photographed by Richard Burbridge
Courtesy Richard Burbridge

**VOGUE**

HAMISH BOWLES
European Editor at Large

*Darling Issie,*

*How we laughed!*

Wickedly fun, visionary, conspiratorial, bawdy, inspirational   how could one do justice to that most life-enhancing phenomenon?

I have a vision of her standing in a new-ploughed field at Hilles, in earnest discussion with the estate manager, who was atop his tractor. She was standing in the muddy waves in brocade Manolos, a coat created by a Japanese protégé and formed of varicolored plastic bags that, when they caught the breeze, billowed out behind her like a birthday child's greedy handful of balloons. Her face was veiled in Philip's scissored gashes of red quills. She was surreal, antic, magnificent.

I have a memory of her arriving at Stroud's Victorian train station, dressed as though for an illicit rendez vous with Trevor Howard in Lee's red and white check Duchess of Windsor suit. And of her then changing, with considerable difficulty, into Lee's bouffant-skirted, leather-harnessed evening dress in the back of the car as it bounded through the lanes en route to a royal Christmas dinner of suckling pig. We made the final adjustments in a glacial field. Issie's necklace spelled BLOW JOB.

I can hear her throaty laugh as its cadences ricocheted around a smoky bistrot on the Boulevard Saint Germain. The mottled mirrors reflected those equine teeth, smudged with scarlet lipstick, some fantastical headdress that bobbed and swayed like a Calder mobile and a dress that appeared to have been fashioned from shards of mirror.

You couldn't have invented Issie. Every moment with her was gala, every moment was a Great Adventure. When she was up she was the essence of life itself.

*Darling, irreplaceable Issie, how I send you more,*

# DITA VON TEESE

## BURLESQUE ARTIST

~~What~~

What if Marlene Dietrich had paid mind to the critics who bashed her controversial but now legendary and often referenced menswear style?

Like Marlene, the adventurous chic of Isabella Blow will not be forgotten. ~~For me, as someone who~~ ~~strives~~ to acheive glamour, mystery, and above all... ~~fun~~ with fashion, Isabella was ~~someone~~ that ~~it~~ was in awe of ~~each time~~ that I saw her, and ~~she continues to inspire me to push myself, to~~ dare to be different, and it was my great privilage to know her.

Thank you, Isabella.

# DANIEL KLAJMIC

**FASHION PHOTOGRAPHER**

São Paolo, Brazil

Nov. 5th, 2009

Having met Isabella really changed my life.

Not only she discovered me, and put my work on the map,

But, she also showed me a way to relate with the world.

She was in love with Beauty, in all its forms.

She was always searching for it, and craving for

that feeling, that warm sensation we get when we are

touched by a beautiful image.

She taught me to look for it, everywhere.

Thank you, Izzy, with all my heart!

Sincerely,

Daniel Klajmic

# JUERGEN TELLER

## PHOTOGRAPHER

Issabella Blow

It was end of the eighties, and I can't remember, but somehow I had an appointment with Izzy at Tatler. She seen my work, so I went, nervous, still hardly could speak english. I couldn't believe what I was seeing! A totally excentric, to me weird looking, charming woman. First thing I noticed was her lipstick stain on her teeth. Anyway, after looking at my work enthusiasticly at my work, she ask me to come into this small room at the fashion department of Tatler. She looke locked the door behind her and started to undress her top and all this english white fleshy breast came out, I was pushed in a corner. I stood there like a 12 year old frightened boy, till someone knocked at the door, Izzy became nervous, put her top back on and opened the door.
That was strange? I remember it was a sunny day. We started working together, but never brought up that weird something ever again X

Isabella Blow with antlers, photographed by Juergen Teller
Courtesy Juergen Teller

44

# SADIE COLES HQ

## LONDON ART GALLERY

Isabella and Detmar joined us on the Greek Island of Hydra in summer 2001 for the annual art weekend of collector and patron Pauline Karpidas. Hydra is a quiet and relaxing island, with a beautiful harbour for visiting yachts and day-trippers from Athens, and has been a haven for glamorous visitors and residents since the sixties. But Hydra hadn't seen anything like Isabella before. She disembarked from the ferry, with an impressive suitcase count for a two night stay, in striking sunglasses and arresting décolletage, clutching Seamus Heaney's Electric Light and teetering about on the cobblestones in the highest stilettos. Finding the island had no taxis, only mules, Isabella established an elegantly imperious way of sitting on one for her journeys to the hotel, the restaurant, the bar, the monastery at the top of the mountain, and to the little beach taverna where we had lunch. Her bright red lipstick never faded, she never made it from the taverna to the beach, and she never stopped talking about the island called Lesbos. And on the way back to London Isabella kindly sent a glass of champagne from business class to Detmar in economy, who promptly returned it.

Sadie Coles and Pauline Daly

Isabella Blow, 2004, photographed by T J Wilcox
Courtesy T J Wilcox and Sadie Coles HQ

" VISIONARY, CONSPIRATORIAL,
BAWDY, INSPIRATIONAL;
YOU COULDN'T HAVE INVENTED ISSY "

**HAMISH BOWLES**

# ALICE RAWSTHORN

## DESIGN CRITIC INTERNATIONAL HERALD TRIBUNE

I should have known that if anyone was going to haunt me it would be Issy. And, although I'm not at all sure where I stand on the supernatural, I think she probably has.

It happened when I returned to London from a weekend at Hilles, the Blow family home that Issy had adopted and loved as her own. It was a year-and-a-half after her death, and I went back for the first time since her funeral tea for a dinner that Detmar was throwing for a mutual friend, Gregor Muir.

I'd thought about Issy all weekend, feeling more and more uneasy about being at Hilles without her. The following day I was sorting through some papers in my office, and emptied the contents of a box where I put notes, letters and mementoes that I want to save. I picked up a thick clump of papers to reveal a Stefan Brüggemann[1] portrait of Issy in what looked like a Red Indian headdress, roaring with laughter as she stuck out her tongue. "Gotcha!" she seemed to be saying. "Did you really think you could go to Hilles without me?"

When I mentioned this to a physicist friend he scoffed at the suggestion that it might be anything more than a coincidence. The scientific explanation, or so he said, is a syndrome called "selective attention" whereby we find ourselves noticing people, things, sounds, smells or images from the thousands of things we see – but generally fail to notice – every day for the simple reason that we've been thinking about them.

Sure, I said, it couldn't be purely coincidental to have found myself face-to-face with Issy the day after visiting her old home. Oh yes it was, he said firmly. But he wasn't lucky enough to know my wonderful, strong, passionate, witty, irrepressible and, often, very silly friend, Issy.

[1] The image by Stefan Brüggemann to which Alice Rawsthorn refers features on page 67

FACING PAGE: Isabella Blow, photographed by Roxanne Lowit

Courtesy Roxanne Lowit

# EBE OKE

**MUSICIAN**

Isabella was an otherworldly creature of mythical proportions. She was for me the personification of an artistic ideal that I had had since I was a child and she completely captivated my imagination during the years I knew her. It was the experimental music that I had crafted from bird sounds, sampled on the farm I grew up on in South Georgia, that broke the ice. The natural dichotomies within us forged an instant friendship. She lived a surreal life and was art made incarnate, a gaping conduit of zeitgeist! I wonder if this was perhaps too much for her to handle. She became like my (wicked) aunt who brayed like a donkey with the most unhinged and haughty laughter.

Isabella believed in my work and pushed me and opened doors for me. She was very loving and generous and was my muse for quite some time. An exotic bird in the city; the most important lesson she taught me was to live life without compromise and with great taste.

Isabella Blow with Ebe Oke
Courtesy Ebe Oke

# NAOMI CAMPBELL

## SUPERMODEL

When I first met Isabella, I was almost fifteen years old; she was working with Michael Roberts at the time. Issy always seemed to introduce me to, or have me work with, the latest rising star – such as David LaChapelle.

I recall one time in New York, in David's studio, when Issy was preparing to get a plane (British Airways) back to London. Never had any airline in the world seen a woman so chic and elegant. She was dressed in a real masterpiece creation by Lee McQueen, accompanied by the most incredible hat and of course her signature red lipstick. It was a pure vision.

I said to her: "Issy, are you going to change on the plane to sleep?" She looked at me and replied: "This is very comfortable, and I shall not remove a thing."

Issy, you will always be a huge inspiration to me and many people around the world. May you rest in peace.

Isabella Blow, photographed by Miguel Reveriego

Courtesy Miguel Reveriego

# VICTORIA BECKHAM

**POP SINGER / FASHION DESIGNER**

David and I first met Isabella at Sam Taylor Wood and Jay Joplin's house. Isabella was wearing what she referred to as her "Polo Mint" hat.

David said to Isabella: "I like your HAT," to which she replied: "Thank you; everything good comes with a hole." David was astounded and never forgot what she said that night, on our first meeting!

A few months later I invited Isabella to watch David play at Old Trafford. She wore a hat that Philip had made for his *Pop Art* couture show in Paris 2003, featuring a portrait of David in an "Andy Warhol" style.

I'll always remember the most extraordinary entrance Isabella made into the players' lounge. She epitomized Old Hollywood glamour in a leather jacket, pencil skirt, fishnet tights and crazy high heels. Old Trafford has never, and will never, see such glamour again.

Isabella Blow wearing the "Polo Mint" hat, 2003, photographed by Dominic O'Neill
Courtesy Dominic O'Neill

# VALENTINO

## FASHION LEGEND

I think she was nervous every time she met me. She told me that my eyes were like x rays. She said that I examined her from top to toe and in my mind probably I was shocked by her attire.

Not at all. Mine was just an admiration for the artist; for the courageous woman; for the inspiration to many.

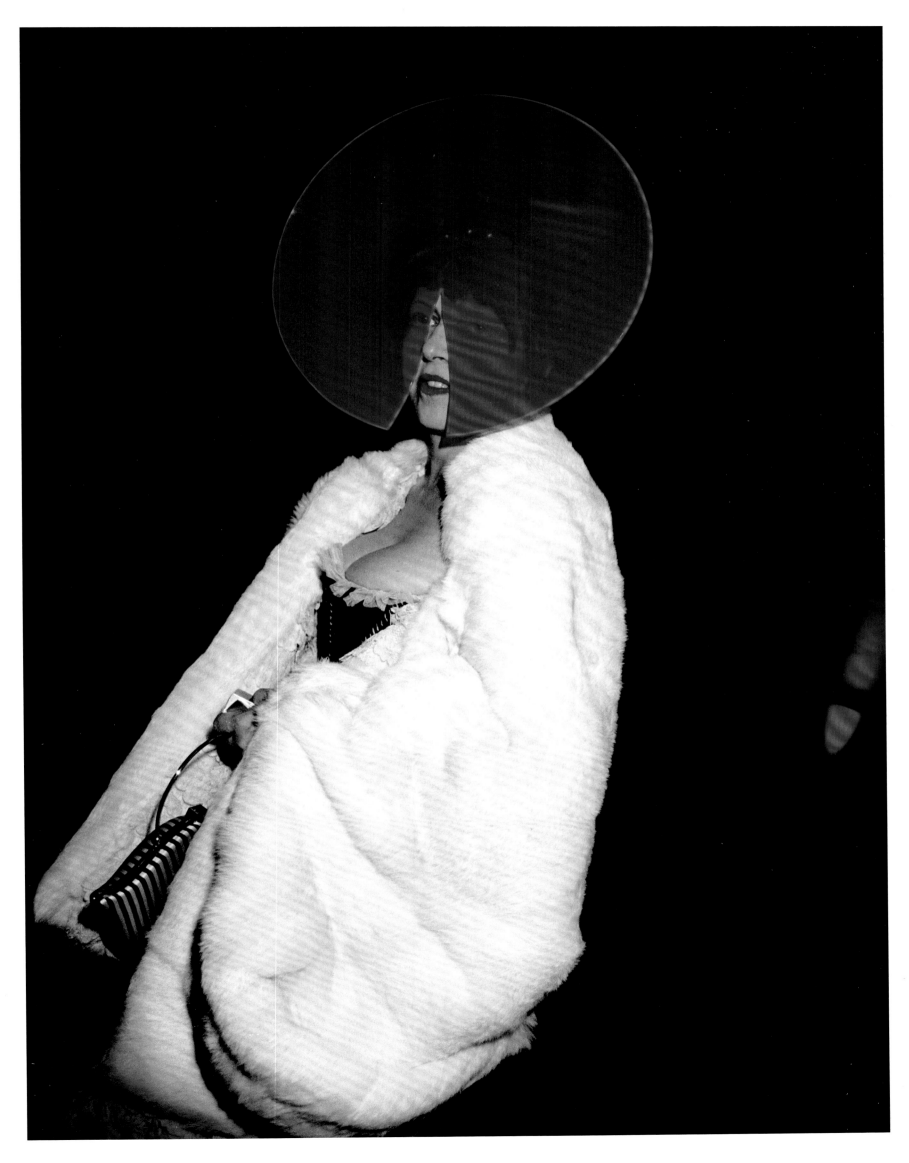

# KEVIN DAVIES

## PHOTOGRAPHER

We were shooting Erin O'Connor for a *Tatler* cover; it was the first time Philip Treacy had shot for the magazine.

Issy knew all the make-up girls in London's department stores. On a normal day, she'd call in to see them and have her make-up done. If she was going out in the evening, she'd drop by late in the afternoon and have them do her face. Then she would arrive looking terrific, as if she'd spent all day getting ready. In fact, she was a very hard-working, industrious person.

I was fascinated by that style she had, of looking like she was lounging around doing nothing, when in fact she was getting the job done, extremely well. The serious gentleman in the foreground is guarding a million pounds worth of diamonds, which are draped on Erin, out of shot.

FACING PAGE AND FOLLOWING SPREAD: Isabella Blow at work, photographed by Kevin Davies
Courtesy Kevin Davies

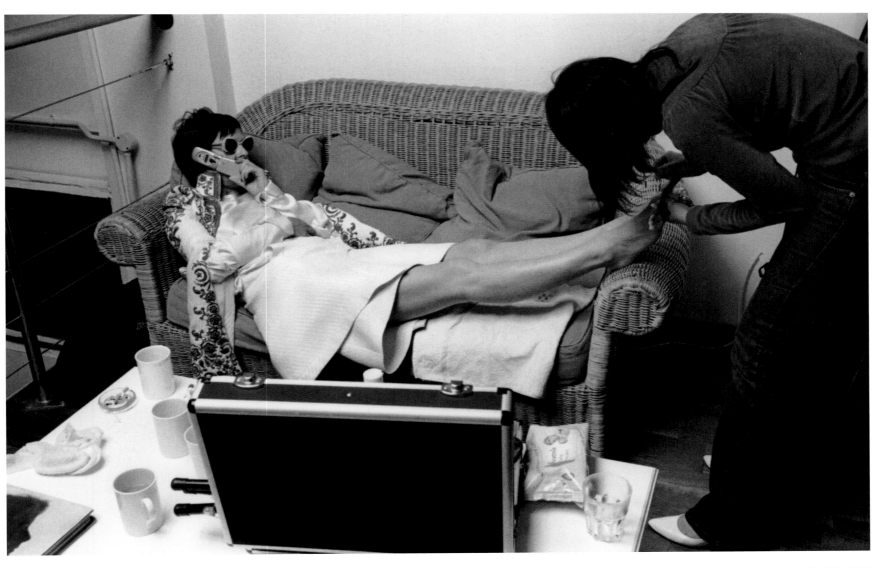
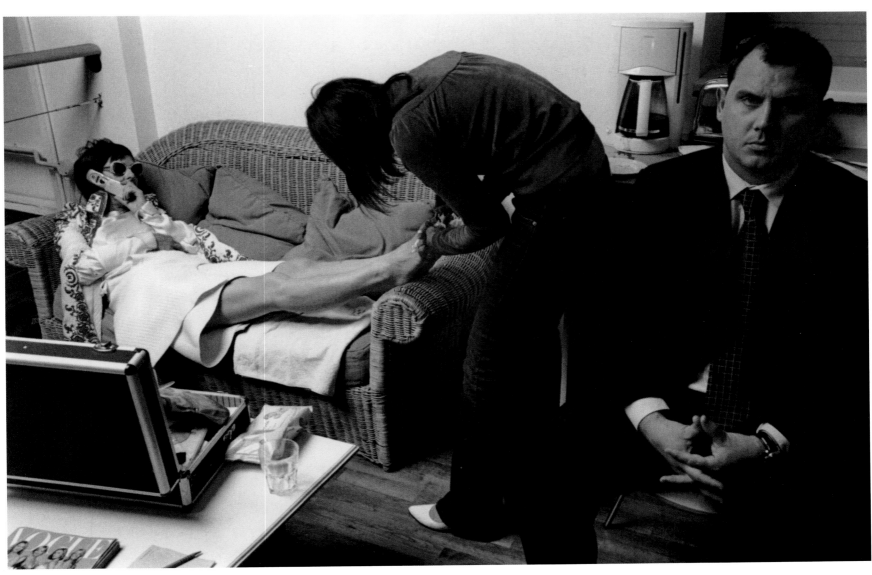

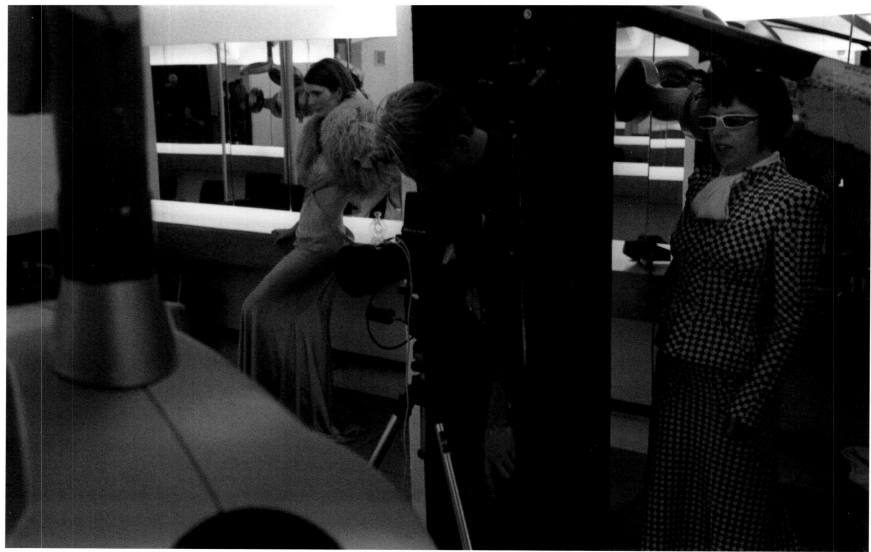

# STEFAN BRÜGGEMANN

**ARTIST**

13 WORDS FOR ISABELLA BLOW

1. (ABSTRUSE)

2. (SPEED)

3. (ROMANCE)

4. (VEXEDLY)

5. (ALTRUISM)

6. (BEYOND)

7. (DEJECTION)

8. (LOOK)

9. (EXTRAORDINARY)

10. (MOUTH)

11. (ELEGANT)

12. (LAUGH)

13. (NO)

STEFAN BRÜGGEMANN 2010

Isabella at her desk, photographed by Stefan Brüggemann
Courtesy Stefan Brüggemann

# HARRIET VERNEY

## ISABELLA'S NIECE

"Fashion is about eventually getting naked."
*Vivienne Westwood*

Issy would wrap you up in a Treacy and McQueen limited edition way. We were constantly playing dress-up with and secretly without her. One time I stole her polaroid camera to take pictures of myself and my friends in her clothes; the next day she found the pictures but instead of getting angry she put them in an envelope and sent them off to Sarah Doukas at Storm.

On the rare occasion when our whole family were together, Issy would be there; the last time was at Bryan Ferry's concert in Oxford. We all travelled up in two cars, with Issy's competitive streak shown by her demanding we race the other car there. Once we had arrived, Issy took to being the centre of attention – standing up and whipping her scarf in the air with patent gold trousers; standing on the chairs; she was the first to run to the front to dance, and the last one to care.

And the last thing she asked me? For a jersey cow, milkmaid included.

Isabella Blow, photographed by Sean Ellis
Courtesy Sean Ellis

" I SHOULD HAVE KNOWN
THAT IF ANYONE
WAS GOING TO HAUNT ME
IT WOULD BE ISSY "

**ALICE RAWSTHORN**

THE DESIGN MUSEUM IN LONDON WERE
PUTTING TOGETHER A TOURING EXHIBITION
ENTITLED "WHEN PHILIP MET ISABELLA"
MOSTLY MADE UP OF THE COLLECTION OF
PHILIP TREACY HATS AND FASHION PHOTOGRAPHS,
ISSY PERSUADE US TO CONTRIBUTE A
PORTRAIT OF HER, WE'D ALWAYS RESISTED
THE LURE TO DO PORTRAITS OF ANYONE ELE,
ANDY WARHOL STYLE, EXCEPT FOR I THINK,
A PAIR OF 'FUCKING RATS'.
WE AGREED ON THIS OCCASION, AND SO
ISSY DUMPED ON US BOXFULS OF PERSONAL
ITEMS, MANOLO BLAHNIK'S AND HER ICONIC
KILLER RED LIPSTICKS ETC. (SOME OF WHICH
WERE FAR TOO GOOD TO DESTROY - I KEPT
FOR MYSELF) PLUS OTHER SUCH STUFF WE
DEEMED TOO 'FLUFFY' TO USE... ANY
PORTRAIT OF ISSY SHOULD NOT BE MADE OF
'SUGAR AND SPICE AND ALL THINGS NICE',
BUT THE DARKER SIDE OF LIFE - IN THIS
INSTANCE WE SOURCED A HANDFUL OF
MATERIALS WE FELT SUITED THIS GOTHIC
STYLE - A RAVEN FROM THE
TOWER OF LONDON AND A BLACK RAT
FROM THE PLAGUE...

*[signatures]* SUE WEBSTER.

Tim Noble & Sue Webster, *The Head Of Isabella Blow*, 2002
15 taxidermy animals (1 rattlesnake, 1 raven, 1 robin, 6 magpies, 2 hooded crows, 1 carrion crow, 2 rooks, 1 black rat),
wood, fake moss, light projector, installation template, courtesy the artists

# TRACEY EMIN

## ARTIST

We had been travelling on a night
Flight from London to Athens. This
was back in the 90's when Brit Art was
very rough travel. I sat at the ferry port
port of Pireaus, as the sun was rising,
my head in my hands with an incredible
hangover. Isabella stood there immaculate
in a white flimsy mac, the highest most
painful shoes in the world, eyelashes longer
than the branches of a tree, bright red lips,
hand on hip looking triumphant.

I said "for Christ's sake Issy - cant
you just give it a rest" She turned round
Looked at me, and without a trace of irony
Said "give what a rest?"

Brilliant, brilliant! In my mind
She remains a brilliant, brilliant
woman.

*Tracey Emin 08*

# HILARY KNIGHT

## FASHION ILLUSTRATOR

LEFT: Philip Treacy adjusts the "Opium Den" on Isabella, by Hilary Knight
RIGHT: Isabella at Hilles, sharing the family album, February 1998, by Hilary Knight
Courtesy Hilary Knight

Feb 1998

At "Hilles" Detmar Blow + Isabellas

In black egret by Tracy

Isabella shares with weekend
guests the family album

Photo of Grandmother +
Grandfather ("White Mischief")

# PAUL SMITH

**DESIGNER**

What impressed me about Isabella
was that whenever I met her at a private view
or party with my wife, she always remembered
Pauline's name and engaged in a conversation with her,
unlike most people who were only interested in talking to me.
Isabella was a very special person.

Paul Smith

Paul Smith

" ISABELLA WAS AN
OTHERWORLDLY CREATURE
OF MYTHICAL PROPORTIONS "

EBE OKE

# SARAH DOUKAS

## FOUNDER OF STORM MODEL AGENCY

Storm has lost a great friend. I first met Issy in 1985 or 1986 through one of my male models Tim Hunt — he was the Ralph Lauren model at the time, and a great friend of Issy's. This was during Issy's time at Vogue. She had fantastic dress sense and at that time always wore bustiers!

My brother Simon and I started a scouting relationship with her in the early 90's, it was very successful. Sophie Dahl being one of the fabulous people she found.

Issy knew everyone. She was so passionate about life and people. My accounts department told me that everytime any of them saw Issy out of our office she always greeted them + had time for them.. That is rare + one of her many qualities.

I miss her enormously — she had so many original ideas + dreams +

The world is a sorrier place without her.

height 5'11"/1.80...bust 32d/81...
waist 24/61...hip 36/91...dress 8/10...
shoes 8/41...hair blond...eyes blue...

sophie dahl

# storm®

Storm Model Management, 5 Jubilee Place, London  SW3 3TD
T: 44 020 7376 7764  F: 44 020 7376 5145  www.stormmodels.com

height 5'8.5"/1.74...bust 34a/86...
waist 25/64...hip 35/89...dress 8...
shoes 5/38...hair brown...eyes green...

iris palmer

# storm®

Storm Model Management, 5 Jubilee Place, London  SW3 3TD
T: 44 020 7376 7764  F: 44 020 7376 5145  www.stormmodels.com

# SOPHIE DAHL

**MODEL / AUTHOR**

Big laugh
Bigger heart
Red lips
Tuberose Scented
Clattering heels
Beloved
Marvellous
Inimitable
Isabella

♡
Sophie D.

Sophie Dahl wearing a Philip Treacy hat, photographed by David LaChapelle
Courtesy David LaChapelle

# ANNA PIAGGI

## ITALIAN FASHION ICON

Isabella Blow represented, for me,
a regally spontaneous eccentricity.
Even trying to write about her
encourages me to think paradoxical, quizzical, unheard of,
even contradictory in words,
but always
with a very sentimental feeling.
Seeing and meeting her
was always
a tender choc,
a touching taste
of invention
and, many times,
the outrageous left place,
from my part,
to an unconditioned admiration.
Our difference of age
(she was much younger than me)
created, particularly through
some late "fashion seasons,"
a very surprising rapport.
It was like she wanted
to protect me,
to take care of me:
she was worried
that I lived alone
and I had to reassure her
that I was used to that.
She was finding it
rather surprising
and I was, in a way,
very much touched.
I admired her very much
for her consistency
as a stylist-editor in chief
of *Tatler*,
not only deriving from her personal style
but also, certainly, from a "métier formidable"
in editorial technique.
About the collaboration
with Philip Treacy
she was infusing her taste
in a mutual exchange
of ideas and she was always
a directional source
of inspiration,
exuding poetry and literature.
And again, paradoxically,
never so much
as at her Memorial.
Seen, from the entrance
of the Guards Chapel,
the profiles of the ladies heads
represented Her!
Ah! The hats, the black silhouettes,
the elegance…
I will never forget.
Fashion as the most beautiful
and elegant theatre in life.
And the last "adieu"
of Isabella as in a whirl of feathers.
Real? Unreal?

Isabella Blow with Anna Piaggi
Courtesy Anna Piaggi

# SHAUN LEANE

## JEWELLERY DESIGNER

As I walked into the private view, I heard the sound of a dear friend. A deep laughter, with depth and character. Before I saw the hat I smelt Fracas - a scent that warms my heart. A smile graced my face to know my friend Issy was there.

I walked the room, said hello to a few, with great anticipation to end up having Issy all to myself. It was when the fun would begin. Issy and I embraced, so glad to see each other. Having her there made the evening worthwhile.

This particular evening I remember, we were both like mischevous children as if trying out our first drops of alcohol. We wanted to smoke but the street was many levels below. So like naughty school children, we huddled into a secret corner to share a quick cigarette. Giggling, whilst lighting the cigarette, we were spotted by security. We were told to put the cigarette out but found the whole thing quite hilarious. We ran to the lift while being chased by the guard. The more he chased the more we laughed. We waved goodbye to the security guard as the lift doors closed and descended down to the street, where we ran arm in arm laughing out loud. It was like reliving ones childhood.

We then proceeded to Claridges where we wined and dined and talked about all things beautiful.

I have many wonderful memories of Issy but this one sticks in my mind for some reason, maybe because as we ran and laughed we didn't have a care in the world.

Shaun

TOP: Isabella Blow wearing "Hook my Heart" necklace by Shaun Leane, with Shaun and Elton John (photographed at Shaun Leane's launch party for the black diamond "Hook my Heart" collection at Liberty, 2004)

BOTTOM: Bracelet made by Shaun Leane for Isabella Blow, courtesy Shaun Leane

# BRYAN FERRY

## MUSIC LEGEND

There was never a dull moment with Isabella — she had a marvellous sense of humour, and the most infectious laugh, which could be heard for miles!

TOP: Portrait of Bryan Ferry
BOTTOM: Bryan Ferry with Isabella and Detmar Blow, courtesy Bryan Ferry

# ROBERT ASTLEY SPARKE

## PHOTOGRAPHER

ISSY PUSHED BUTTONS IN PEOPLE
THAT THEY MAY HAVE NOT DARED
TO PUSH THEMSELVES. SHE LOVED
MUDDLING THINGS UP WHICH WAS PART
OF HER BRILLIANCE. HER THOUGHTS WERE
SO ABSTRACT SOMETIMES. I MISS THE
LAUGHS WE HAD TOGETHER TRYING TO
WORK OUT WHAT THEY MEANT.

ISSY, THERE WERE SO MANY WONDERFUL
TIMES, FUN & HAPPY DAYS. YOU WERE
SO KIND, HUMBLE, GRACIOUS AND HELPFUL
TO SO MANY.

ALWAYS MISSING & LOVING YOU

Robert
x

FACING PAGE AND FOLLOWING SPREAD: Stills from "Nipples from Naples" photo shoot for *Tatler* by Robert Astley Sparke,
styled by Isabella Blow, art directed by Leon St Amour, courtesy Robert Astley Sparke, Leon St Amour and Condé Nast
BOTTOM RIGHT: Isabella Blow takes the lead for the image that appeared on the opening spread

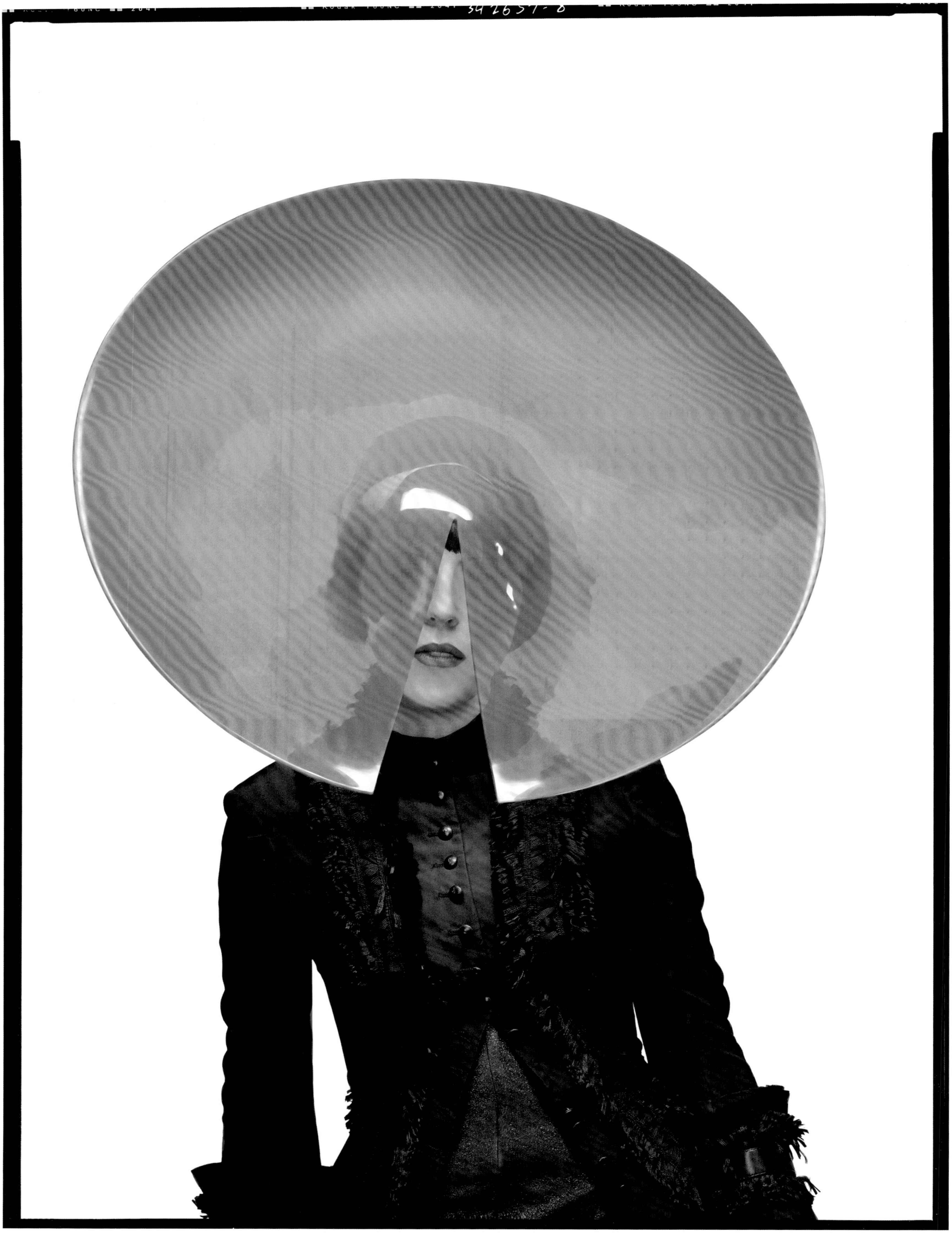
342657-8

# RICHARD SORGER

**FASHION DESIGNER**

I first met Isabella in Sept. '06 at ON/OFF where I was exhibiting my first RTW collection. Within seconds of arriving at my stand she informed me that she wanted me to make her some stockings she could 'get fucked in' and then insisted that I feel the metal plate in her (bare) feet.

A few weeks later I asked her if she'd give a talk at Middlesex University where I lecture part-time. She agreed as long as I interviewed her on stage. She sent me a book of Francis Bacon interviews as a reference.

On the day, she arrived in McQueen hat that looked like roadkill. She charmed all the staff and students and then set off all the fire alarms by smoking in my office! On stage, just before we started she confessed that she was really nervous, now confronted by the huge audience and I was rather endeared that this fascinating woman would feel like this. She needn't have worried – she was captivating and wonderfully indiscreet about some very famous people.

Photographs from Chris Moore's archive
Courtesy Chris Moore / Catwalking

# GILES DEACON

**FASHION DESIGNER**

After so many visits to the Studio
from Issy, so many fantastic memories
were formed. The image here is a
particularly good one. Issy had asked
for a new season dress to wear to the
show, so a "Issy for giles" was duly
made. A very excited Issy left up before
the show had finished and became
the last look! Pure genius issy.

giles
x.

Isabella Blow takes centre-stage at the close of the Giles Deacon Spring / Summer 2007 catwalk show during London Fashion Week, 2006
Stills from video footage by Chris Moore, courtesy Chris Moore and Giles Deacon

" SHE WAS UNSTOPPABLY
EXTRAVAGANT;
EVEN HER JOKES WERE
EXPENSIVE "

**LIZA CAMPBELL**

# PRASHANT VERMA

## FASHION DESIGNER

*"An artist is a person who has invented an artist."*
Harold Rosenberg, *Discovering the Present*, 1974

I write this for Isabella Blow as the world mourns the death of Alexander McQueen.

Isabella Blow was a fountain of dust, held together with the glue of mythical madness so few have the fortune of experiencing. A flower that could pierce and explode. A flower that roared like a lion. A rose as red as blood, armoured by a thousand thorns.

Isabella was. And Isabella was not. Who she was, and who we saw, perhaps were not the same. The Philip Treacy headpiece, the Alexander McQueen dress, the Fracas fragrance, and the eyes – that gaze that struck you like the gargoyles that guarded her fortress – perhaps in there, deep inside her castle – there was no one else – deep inside . . . therein was the mystery that was Isabella Blow.

Isabella was beautiful dark matter. Isabella created a visual we all called "Isabella Blow." A façade, an escape route, a canvas, an armour – one she exploded on, one that she constantly hid behind. In reality she was not Isabella Blow. But she created and lived that lie. In that, it was the absolute truth.

History bears evidence time and again of how we overlook the truth and reasons behind the fantasy that many like her have lived out. A fantasy that takes us away from our suffering and internal conflicts. In running away from such demons, in facing the ticking bombs, in staring at life . . . I recall our last cryptic telephonic conversation on the subject of life, light, darkness and love . . . when we spoke of minotaurs and warriors . . . I recall her voice as she said to me . . . "your insecurity is your key."

It's true. We are our own devil.[1]

[1] Quoted from "Paradise Circus" by Massive Attack, on the album *Heligoland*, 2010

FACING PAGE: Isabella Blow with Prashant Verma, courtesy Vishesh Verma

# FRANCA SOZZANI

## EDITOR-IN-CHIEF VOGUE ITALY

Isabella was a "unicum," a one-off, a singular woman. None could be like her. She was naturally eccentric. No effort. She couldn't be different. Her attitude, her allure made her special, as well of course as the unique way she dressed and wore incredible hats; hats that only she could wear. When she was laughing she was like a little girl. She was funny and ironic. Creative and extravagant. She was able to recognize talented people. She introduced me to Philip Treacy and Alexander McQueen, and when both of them became very famous she was happy as their success was her own. She was generous. A real friend. Photographers loved to take portraits of her and in every photo she looked absolutely stunning. Her natural creative craziness made her different from anyone else and her style could never be duplicated or imitated. When someone tries to copy her eccentricity, the result is a dull imitation.

For me her image is frozen the night she arrived for dinner at the Connaught Hotel with Philip Treacy and Stefan Bartlett. The trio was absolutely unique in their elegance and extravagancy. The contrast between them and the formal restaurant was like a theatrical performance. It was a vision. She was laughing and kidding with my son, calling him "my beautiful Romeo." At any of the events I organized since then she was the first one to be invited. Still today I think of her, I miss her at the shows and I miss her asking: "How is Romeo?"

Isabella Blow, photographed by Steven Meisel
Selected by Franca Sozzani, courtesy Steven Meisel

# LUCY BIRLEY

## FORMER MODEL / LONDON SOCIALITE

Isabella, sparkling like a comet
hooded lids lowered in conspiracy,
a chuckle, a snort,
a fan of quivering feathers.

Isabella, a flash of red, a laugh, a squeeze.
Sweet scent wafts across the boards,
you totter in a goatskin skirt
behind you flickering flames
as your love of flesh curls your lip.

A warrior for England,
armoured, corsetted, ready.
Your imagination soaring to the plains of India,
a row of diamond daisies twinkle under lace,
on a train across China.
Isabella, your hungry eye a spark
to light the fuse of so many lives.

On Fifth Avenue your silver skirt blows
in the hot wind,
white-legged you stride across the moor.
Breaking ice, cutting through with your rapier held high,
in strict black satin.
The dead house revives and crackles alight.
Jangling, tripping, snorting, you console all but yourself.

Isabella, you held the blueish liquid to your lips in triumph,
at the birth of spring.
The cage door swung open
lifting you to the clouds;
below a darkened storm of tears,
on the ramparts a pyre of embroidered silks,
your glittering finger clock ticks on.

All is dull, silent, without you.

FACING PAGE AND FOLLOWING SPREAD: Interior of Isabella Blow's London apartment
Photographed by Fritz von der Schulenburg ©THE WORLD OF INTERIORS

" SHE WAS A TRUE SELF-DESTRUCTIVE

BIG-HEARTED ECCENTRIC "

**HUSSEIN CHALAYAN**

# MARCUS TOMLINSON

## PHOTOGRAPHER

It was always a great experience working with Issy.

On one occasion, during a shoot with Tim Noble + Sue Webster, Issy turned to me and asked in an utterly matter of fact manner whilst in complete earshot of all "Why do all my assistants have such Big Breasts!" Which was particularly shocking to the one who was on her first day.

Issy was more than likely largely judged by her outspoken, offbeat + flamboyant ways. Maybe so much so that it was a wonderful surprise to be caught up in her Big heart of gold. She had an easy intimacy that could build a relationship with someone in a moment.

I often think of when she sent me the most wonderful card when my own father died.

Issy brought the world to life in a way that very few people can...... ... She is truly missed and never forgotten.

Marcus.

# LOUISE WILSON

**HEAD OF MA FASHION CENTRAL ST MARTINS**

Arriving late for the MA central saint mawtins shew in '92 Isabella insisted she sit on the floor! it was here she first saw lee mqveens walk & the next day she met him at the college to buy his collection — 'the rest is hishry'

GIVENCHY

AG39

# RUI LEONARDES

## FASHION DESIGNER

Issie called me after seeing photos of my graduation collection. She wanted to meet me immediately.
It was fashion week, and I was showing a small film that day, I asked if she would like to come, she said: "Dahling I have nothing to wear!!! I will try, but can you come tomorrow morning for breakfast?" — yeah!! sure, I will be there — I thought she was taking the piss.

She came to the show and she wanted all the masks that my friend Manuel Albarran made for the collection, and she wanted it NOW!!!.
After the show she invited me for drinks at her house with some of her friends. Next morning I went back to her house for breakfast. With a hangover the size of China all the masks and collection propped in two Ikea bags — "Dahling you are late!! I made you pancakes with orange" — I felt like I was having an audience with the Queen, but she was so funny and lovely.

She commissioned some footwear, and since that moment my phone didn't stop ringing, it could be 3, 4, 5, 6, 7 am. — "Dahling!!! I have nothing to wear!!! I need you to glue me a pain of kitten heels into a pair of McQueen socks to wear with this Pollini dress that Rifat just sent me.... and, its for tonight!!! Get in a cab a.s.a.p. — I have nothing to wear!!!

Many breakfasts, Lunches, dinners, bottles of gin, vodka and champ followed and we became friends.
She introduced me to amazing people. She guided me, gave me lots of advice. Genuinely she had the best interest in me. She was like a big sister, and I miss her very, very, very much.
xxx Rui

" FOR ME ISABELLA WAS WHAT
FASHION WAS ALL ABOUT
AND YOU CAN'T BE HUMOURLESS
WITH A LOBSTER ON YOUR HEAD "

**BOY GEORGE**

# ELLEN VON UNWERTH

**PHOTOGRAPHER**

Isabella was and is a big inspiration. Not only was she brilliantly funny and entertaining, but she also kept you holding your breath each time she arrived at a party or a fashion show with her eccentric looks.

Working with her was a unique experience, and I miss seeing this wonderful bird of paradise.

Isabella Blow wearing the "Pheasant" hat designed by Philip Treacy, photographed by Ellen von Unwerth
Courtesy Ellen von Unwerth

# BOY GEORGE

## MUSIC ICON

I didn't officially meet Isabella Blow until I started wearing Philip Treacy's incredible hats but I knew of her for years and saw her at every fabulous party and fashion event.

I was always quite wary of her because her reputation was as colossal as some of the hats she wore. I heard endless stories or urban myths about Isabella and was led to believe that she was a ruthless and humourless fashion addict who would cut you dead for wearing the wrong shoes, but once I got to know her I discovered what a hoot she was. For me Isabella was what fashion was all about, and you can't be humourless when you've got a jewel-encrusted lobster perched on your head.

I was coming back from a DJ trip in Germany and as I walked to the baggage hall I found myself all alone on one of those never-ending walkways at Terminal 1. Suddenly in the distance I could see a vision coming the other way and as we got closer I could see it was Isabella and she was wearing this massive lace cone creation on her head, which I knew would go down well in first class. "Oh my God," I said, "I'm loving this comfortable travelling look you're working; are you on your own?"

I can't think of many people who would be brave enough to catch a flight alone dressed like that, but Isabella seemed to live in an alternative universe at times and while I'm sure she relished the stares and gasps, she never never let it get in the way of her commitment to style. She was like Leigh Bowery in the sense that you never really knew where she was going to take it next but she always took it somewhere surreal and fabulous. I still can't believe that she's gone and I can't imagine we will ever see the likes of her again. Like Bowery she was totally unique and iconic and will be remembered for years to come.

# SEAN ELLIS

## FASHION PHOTOGRAPHER / FILM DIRECTOR

In 1995 my phone rang and a posh voice shouted "I love your crotch shots." It was a reference to a shoot I had done for *Dazed and Confused*.

"Who's that?" I asked.

"It's Issy Blow." And so started my relationship with Issy. She didn't do things by halves and if there's a single word to describe her it would be "impact." We shared the same sense of humour and always talked about life in terms of war. "Fashion is a battleground," she used to say, normally followed by: "We'll show the bastards!" We both felt a great need to do something that would last. Our shoots together were often long, intense, labours of love but for commercial campaigns Issy was always hilarious: "What the fuck are we shooting today?" she would say to the client, knowing damn well what we were shooting.

"It's this shirt and these trousers," would come the reply.

"Not very sexy is it?" she said. "Shall we do nudes instead?" And off the client's shocked face she would start her roaring laugh and finish with: "Don't worry it will look great!" Clients loved her. She was always on good form but often her good jokey moods were just like her hats: armour.

I was very sad to hear that Issy had decided to battle no more and hope she can now finally find peace.

The world is less rich without you, Issy.

FACING PAGE: Isabella Blow, photographed by Sean Ellis
FOLLOWING SPREAD: "A Taste of Arsenic," photographed by Sean Ellis, styled by Isabella Blow for *The Face*, 1996
Courtesy Sean Ellis

"BATTLE"

Photo shoot By Sean Ellis for *The Face*
Styled by Isabella Blow
1998

# ANNA WINTOUR

## EDITOR-IN-CHIEF AMERICAN VOGUE

I first met Issy in 1984 when I was American *Vogue*'s Creative Director. I'd been there for six months or so, and I was looking for an assistant. My fellow Brit Brian McNally told me about this fabulously eccentric creature who worked as the coat check girl at one of Ian Schrager's nightclubs. "Anna," Brian said to me, "she would be perfect for you." He was so right. I've always thought that Issy's time at *Vogue* was crucially important to her too. She finally found the sense of purpose that she had been searching for, and it gave her a place where she could show off her considerable talents. Issy also found that the fashion world not only connected with her, but welcomed her with open arms. My feelings about this only grew stronger when I happened to read some letters that Issy had written from America to her dear friend Liza Campbell.

Her letters date from when she lived in Midland Texas with her first husband Nicolas Taylor, to just before she left New York to return to London. I can't for the life of me imagine Issy in Midland; it is not a very fashionable town in a terribly arid and remote part of Texas – the kind of place you drive through to get to somewhere else. I'd have thought that she would have hated it, but Issy's childhood friend Christopher Brooks told me that, for a while at least, she threw herself into Texan life with gusto, joining the local wives, who would go from home to home admiring each others' collections of crystal ornaments. Issy found the whole thing amusing. But then that was typical of her; she had the ability to generate fun, no matter what kind of circumstances she found herself in, as well as an innate empathy with all kinds of different people. Issy also worked while she was in Midland – as an interior decorator, a travel agent, and, when she wrote this in March 1983, as a shop assistant in a local boutique:

"We are leaving this den of doom and heading for New York and I am over the moon," she said. "Please, please could you send me the Piero de Monzi skirt as I have missed it so much, and insure it for £150,000."

I don't know if Issy wore her Piero de Monzi skirt when she came to meet me, but I do remember that she was transfixed by the copy of Vita Sackville West's biography that was on my desk. She said to me: "I've cried each of the three times that I've read it." "Issy," I told her, "there's nothing to cry about." Here is what she wrote about her interview in a letter from February 1984:

"I am waiting all day for Anna Wintour to take me on at *Vogue*. So far I've seen one of the toughest girls in the dizzy world of fashion, but I'm positive if this job doesn't work out she will have elephantine memories of my superb interview. The fashion world is definitely 'me'. I lied like the devil on my resume; I said that I'd been to London University, etc. "

Even if I had known Issy had somewhat stretched the truth, I would still have hired her. She brought such a glorious sense of excitement to the place – not least because of the way she looked. No-one else there wore such short skirts, or came in with runs in their tights, or left their vivid red lipstick on their teeth. She might turn up dressed as the most sumptuous Maharajah, or like Rosalind Russell in *His Girl Friday*. Once she wore an elaborate sari creation that unravelled as she exited the Condé Nast building on Madison Avenue. She didn't notice – or didn't care – and hopped into a cab, only to get the fabric caught in the door. The last anyone saw of Issy that day was the silk sari streaming in the tail wind, heading uptown. Such was her fame around the building that Si Newhouse would make excuses to visit me, just so that he could see what Issy was wearing.

Of course, the truth is that even when she was wearing her sexy 1940s secretary look, Issy was actually far more efficient and capable than the fancy dress would suggest. She could even type, because she'd been to secretarial school at some point in her chequered career history. Dressing up was about making her job into an event. Issy had the most wonderful ability to elevate even the most basic of tasks and turn it into something memorably thrilling. She had no time for anything humdrum, banal, or mundane – to the extent that the task of cleaning her desk every night had to be done with a bottle of Perrier water and Chanel No. 5.

I also found her a joy to have around because she had a new thought or an original observation to make every minute, adding her outrageous laugh for emphasis. There was something very refreshing and liberating about working with someone who immersed herself in worlds that went beyond fashion. She knew a lot of artists in New York, and brought them into the magazine – quite literally; Jean Michel Basquiat would hang around *Vogue* waiting for Issy to finish up so they could go off for dinner. She would help out with shoots, displaying an incredible tenacity to get something really extraordinary out of the ordinary. Issy was asked to find a gym, and there was not a single one to her liking in the whole of Manhattan. So she hired an architect – who had registered his practice in the name of his cat, I recall – to create her idea of the perfect workout space in a warehouse in Queens.

In one of her last letters from New York, she stated: "*Vogue* is like joining the church. It is a whole new perspective on life, and it has done a lot for the yellow fang inferiority complex. I have become quite a megalomaniac instead. The job is not exactly my first choice because I am not in the fashion department, but I do intend to move into the fashion cupboard ASAP."

When she was back in London, she got her wish, of course, working with Michael Roberts at *Tatler*. Then she never got out of the fashion cupboard – and very few people have ever made better use of their time in it. Over the years, whenever she would call me up to urge me to see someone new, I would do it because Issy thought it was important. I'll always remember Michael telling me that Issy had dragged him off to some dingy, godforsaken club in Piccadilly to see the show of her latest discovery, and had excitedly said to him, "Wasn't he fabulous! And the show so unforgettable!" Michael didn't agree – vile, was his estimation – and he told her so. Issy ignored him. She was so thrilled, she'd even had her hair gilded with the designer's name – McQueen – just like the girls in the show.

Just as Issy predicted, our first meeting – as well as our early days together at *Vogue* – always stayed with me. Even in the smallest of ways; when I am interviewing a potential new member of staff, I always ask them what they are reading, and I have yet to come across anyone who was as heartfelt, or as memorable, in their literary preferences as Issy. But more than that, I still put into practice what she helped me understand every single day I work at *Vogue*. Issy believed that culture – and I firmly include fashion, and designers, and magazines in this – should be constantly surprising, and innovative, and inspirational. Yes, she was mercurial in her thinking – just when you thought her antennae were attuned to fashion, you'd suddenly realize that they were now directed towards the contemporary art world. But that was her way: she always wanted to encourage and support whatever was good and new and original. She did it for the love of talent, not self-promotion. Once, I heard that some hapless individual had tried to embroil Issy in a scheme because it would be a way for her to promote herself. "Publicity! Publicity!" she cried, "I need publicity like Jane Eyre needs Mrs. Rochester."

The fashion world has changed so much since we first met in 1984. It has become so global, corporate and, yes, publicity-driven, in its outlook. Yet Issy never forgot what was really important: that, at its best, fashion is all about discovery, and inspiration, and creating magic. And that is why none of us will ever forget her.

Original text from memorial speech 09/18/07
Courtesy Anna Wintour

# SUZY MENKES

## FASHION EDITOR INTERNATIONAL HERALD TRIBUNE

I like to think of Issy as one of the world's great eccentrics. A bit of Edith Sitwell, whom her imperious profile resembled; a touch of the Marchesa Casati, with her dashing style and her grandiose attitude to money. Not an English eccentric you understand, because that phrase is trotted out to belittle exceptional and original talent, and also to minimise the drive and courage it takes to be an original in such a corporate fashion world. I'd like to quote part of a long email that Issy sent me a few weeks before she left us. She was inviting me down to Hilles with Detmar, his family pile, and the subject panel in my computer really said it all: "You have to decide where to put the commas."

"Lolita's hit aristocrats and artists in fertility Stroud valley modern arts and crafty movement tax plan for Hilles to be opened up with English Heritage Isabella hunts literally now."

That was vintage Issy. The email explodes with enthusiastic plans; her admiration for new designers she had discovered; her ideas with Detmar for the gallery; her encounter with a Kazakhstani billionaire with an Oxford degree and the best legs. She even talked about a new couture riding habit she was making. And all this was expressed with Issy's erudition, worn so very lightly.

The first time I met her as Isabella Delves Broughton, I asked if she was from that "Happy Valley" dynasty. This was before the film had brought it all into the open. She blinked in surprise that I had heard of the scandal and then opened her scarlet lips, relishing the chance to tell me all about this decadent colonial heritage. The last time I saw her was in the Condé Nast canteen – not Anna Wintour's carb-free New York watering hole, but Scott's in Mayfair. Over the bank of shellfish I spotted Alex Schulman, Nicholas Coleridge and Madonna, none of them together. But all heads turned in the restaurant as Issy walked in, hat first. She did the rounds with her latest protégé, showing a fantastic ring with an emerald upright between two flanks of white enamel. I never did discover whether the shy young man with her was the amazing photographer she had discovered or the amazing jeweller; it could have been either. All this took place in a minute and a half.

When I went to talk about this tribute with Detmar at Eaton square, that same Philip Treacy hat that Issy had been wearing at the restaurant was hanging on the wall, along with other Schiaparelli soft sculptures. I got tearful thinking of all my encounters with the wunderkammer that was Issy's wardrobe: the noble Alexander McQueen tailoring, the snow-white fur jacket that she once wore over just a corset in one of her madder incarnations. How exotic Issy was in a comformist world, and how deep was her culture. She could tell us that she had a Plantagenet face, and while we were all trying mentally to adjust to the middle-ages, she was planning a medieval shoot, all grey-stoned turrets with a touch of arts and crafts from Hilles; whether shooting swimsuits as a recreation of the Italian world of *La Dolce Vita*, or searching for unveiled beauty in Arabia, Issy possessed an originality that was unique. There have been so many, many tributes, and don't we all wish that those who recognised Issy in retrospect could have encouraged her in life, let alone found her a big bucks career.

Of all these obituaries, the one that impressed me most appeared in the *Art Newspaper*. In quite a brief article, with a photograph of Issy significantly without her trademark hat, young artists told how they were discovered by Issy, and how the introduction that she made for them changed their lives. How proud Issy should have been as someone who changed lives. We know of course about Philip and about Alexander McQueen, but there are so many other people who were touched by Issy, discovered by her, helped by her.

I don't want to be too reverential about Issy now she's gone. I think I will share the beginning of the email. It started like this: "Suzy, it was great to see you yesterday, as I think about you a lot, because you're the only person in the world of fashion who doesn't have to suck arse." Dear Issy, those may not have been your most graceful words, but I do miss so much your honesty, your wit and your honking, suggestive laugh. I have only one regret, and that is that all of us in the fashion family somehow failed to tell Issy how much we loved and admired her, until it was too late for her to hear our sweet words.

Original text from memorial speech 09/18/07
Courtesy Suzy Menkes

# STUART SHAVE

## MODERN ART GALLERY LONDON

### ISABELLA BLOWS LAST WILL & TESTAMENT

Meeting Isabella Blow changed my life. Hardly a day goes by and I dont think of her.

In pondering a suitable epilogue for this publication I immediatly thought back to a long train journey I shared with her back in 1999. Out of boredom we decided to write her last will & testament. Such existential past times were quite the norm with Isabella.

Isabella Blow had no interest in assigning her material posessions in the event of her death, but rather, expressed a visceral list of demands which she expressly asked me to oversee in the event of her departure.

"Firstly!" she commanded "I would like my head decapitated from my body, and buried on the estate of my father. I would like it cut off, as he cut me out of his will." She paused... 'Secondly! I would like my heart cut out, and buried with Detmar at Hilles." ... Another pause... "And quite where I am going to bury my cunt, I havent decided yet."

Isabella Blow was a classic, an individulist and a genius and no one will make me laugh, in the way that she could, ever again

STUART SHAVE

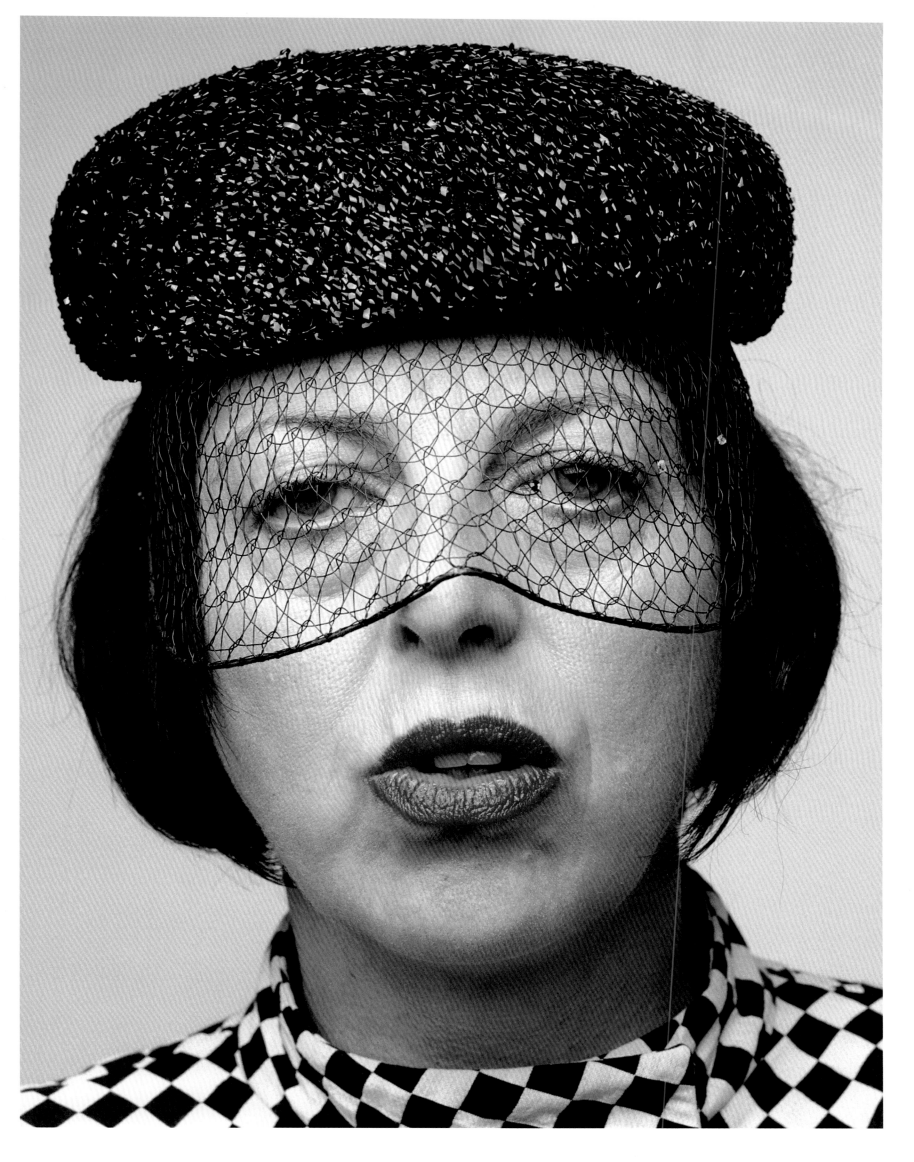

# CONTRIBUTORS

## HILARY ALEXANDER

Hilary Alexander is the Fashion Director of the *Daily Telegraph*, where she has worked for over two decades. In 2001 she was appointed visiting professor at the University of the Arts London and she also holds an Honorary Doctorate in Design from Nottingham Trent University. Alexander appears regularly on UK television and radio broadcasts, including the BBC and Channel 4, and she has been a regular stylist for the reality show *Britain's Next Top Model*.

## VICTORIA BECKHAM

English celebrity Victoria Beckham first rose to fame in the 1990s with pop group the Spice Girls. After the group disbanded she enjoyed a brief solo career, but more recently she has developed into a widely recognised style icon. She has been successful as a fashion designer, appeared in ads for Marc Jacobs and Giorgio Armani, and has launched her own range of sunglasses and a perfume. She is married to footballer David Beckham and resides with her family in Los Angeles.

## STÉPHANE BIESENBACH

Stéphane Biesenbach was born in 1973 in Paris and raised in Germany. From 1995 to 2005 he studied Fine Art in Paris while establishing himself as a freelance illustrator and painter. Since 2005 he has been working as a gallery manager in Berlin.

## LUCY BIRLEY

Lucy Birley is a former model and London socialite who has been captured by photographers such as Robert Mapplethorpe and has been cited as an influence by several major fashion designers. The former wife of Roxy Music lead singer Bryan Ferry, she was the cover model for their album *Avalon*. She is now married to influential businessman Robin Birley.

## MANOLO BLAHNÍK

Forever perpetuated as the God of shoes by the *Sex and the City* franchise, Manolo Blahník's successful career as a shoe designer has spanned over thirty years. Born in the Canary Islands, he later studied in Geneva and Paris before settling in London. He opened his first shop in London's Chelsea in 1973. Decades later he is now a household name and "Manolos" are synonymous with fabulous footwear. Blahník still creates the design and prototype of every single "Manolo" shoe. In 2003 the Design Museum in London hosted a major exhibition of his work and in 2007 Blahník was awarded an Honorary CBE (Commander of the British Empire) in recognition of his achievements.

## HAMISH BOWLES

Having begun his career at *Vogue* in 1992 as Style Editor, Hamish Bowles has been *Vogue*'s European editor-at-large since 1995, and is widely considered to be one of the greatest authorities on fashion and interior design. His current role includes overseeing all celebrity, lifestyle and interior design features within *Vogue*, as well as acting as their liaison to the international fashion markets. Bowles was educated at Central Saint Martins College of Art and Design, and prior to *Vogue* worked at *Harpers and Queen* magazine in London from 1984, as fashion editor. He has also been creative consultant to the Metropolitan Museum of Art.

## STEFAN BRÜGGEMANN

A painting of a rubbish bag by Stefan Brüggemann was aptly placed above the bins in Isabella Blow's Eaton Square flat. Not confined to a single medium, his work includes vinyl, neon, video, painting and installation. Elements of Pop Art are combined with conceptual practice, as Brüggemann balances philosophy with popular culture and sub-culture imagery. He divides his time between London and his native Mexico City and his work has been exhibited at the Kunsthalle, Bern; Museum of Contemporary Art, Chicago; Yvon Lambert Galerie, Paris; Blow de La Barra, London; Bass Museum, Miami, and the Museum of Contemporary Art, Cincinnati.

## RICHARD BURBRIDGE

British photographer Richard Burbridge began his career in the early 1990s and moved to New York in 1993 where he is still based. His well-known work includes editorials for *AnOther Magazine*, *Self-Service*, Italian *Vogue*, *i-D* and *V*, and his still-life and beauty photography can be seen in campaigns for MAC, Chaumet, Givenchy, Hermes and Louis Vuitton Eyewear. A keen interest in science is often reflected in his technically ambitious work.

## NAOMI CAMPBELL

British fashion model Naomi Campbell was first discovered on the streets of London in the 1980s. In August 1988 she became the first black model to appear on the cover of *Vogue* Paris. She established herself as one of the famed supermodels of the 1990s and starred alongside Cindy Crawford in George Michael's famous music video "Freedom." She has also appeared in a number of films, created a range of fragrances and is devoted to charity work, particularly in sub-Saharan Africa.

## DIHONN CARROLL

Dihonn Carroll is a freelance fashion stylist based in London. While studying at the London College of Fashion she gained experience at Channel 4 and the BBC as a make-up artist and wardrobe assistant, before moving on to London Metropolitan University. While studying there she travelled to Milan and Paris with Martina Rink during the fashion weeks, and it was in Milan that she first got to know Isabella Blow. Her freelance work has involved numerous projects in London and has more recently taken her to Los Angeles.

## HUSSEIN CHALAYAN

When Hussein Chalayan graduated from London's Central Saint Martins School of Art and Design in 1993 his entire collection was bought by high-end fashion boutique Browns. A year later he launched his own label and was named British Designer of the Year in 1999 and 2000. He represented Turkey in the 2005 Venice Biennale, with the film *Absent Presence*, starring Tilda Swinton. The film was shown in his major retrospective at London's Design Museum 2009.

## SOPHIE DAHL

Sophie Dahl began her career as a successful model and was photographed by major photographers such as Steven Meisel and David LaChapelle. Writing was always her first love and her first novel *Playing with the Grown-Ups* was published in eight languages. Her bestselling illustrated novella *The Man with the Dancing Eyes* was published in nine languages. She now lives in London, having spent eight years in New York.

## SADIE COLES AND PAULINE DALY

Sadie Coles and Pauline Daly are the Directors of Sadie Coles HQ, a contemporary art gallery in London representing cutting-edge artists such as Matthew Barney, Sarah Lucas and Elizabeth Peyton. In the early 1990s they worked together at Anthony d'Offay and the two met Isabella Blow when she was involved in the gallery Modern Art, founded by Stuart Shave and Detmar Blow.

## KEVIN DAVIES

Kevin Davies' first job was for the British music magazine *NME*, and he soon began working for *i-D* and *The Face*. As a photographer he has often collaborated with Philip Treacy and his work includes fashion and reportage as well as celebrity portraits, landscapes, interiors and still-lifes. He was born in London and has a Fine Art degree from Winchester School of Art.

## GILES DEACON

A graduate of Central Saint Martins College of Art and Design in London, Giles Deacon worked as a designer at Bottega Veneta and the Gucci group for several years before launching his own label, Giles, in 2003. Later that year he was voted Best New Designer at the British Fashion Awards. The collection was featured in prominent fashion publications and was bought by Harvey Nichols, Liberty and Selfridges. Deacon has also designed for high street retailer New Look and is an established illustrator.

## JULIA DELVES BROUGHTON

Julia Delves Broughton is Isabella Blow's younger sister. She currently lives in London and works at Christie's, where she is a director in the Chairman's Office.

## SARAH DOUKAS

Sarah Doukas is the founder of Storm Modelling Agency and represents some of the world's leading fashion models including Kate Moss and Lily Cole. Doukas first started the business in 1987 from her tiny house in London's Battersea. She has since earned a reputation for her excellent ability to spot new talent, and famously discovered Kate Moss at JFK airport in 1988. When Isabella Blow discovered English model Sophie Dahl she promptly referred her to Doukas.

## SEAN ELLIS

Photographer and filmmaker Sean Ellis was born in Brighton and moved to London in his early twenties to pursue a career in fashion photography. His work has appeared in magazines such as *The Face, Dazed & Confused*, British, American, French and Japanese *Vogue* and his style was often described as "cinematic." He soon moved into making music videos, commercials and short films. In 1999 he published his first book of photographs, *365: A Year in Fashion*, and in 2006 his short film *Cashback* was nominated for an Academy Award. He has also been nominated for a BAFTA and has been honoured at film festivals worldwide.

## TRACEY EMIN

A superstar of the Young British Artist Group, Tracey Emin is a staple of London's fashion and art social circles. Emin is famous for her multimedia art that uses her own personal life for inspiration and was a Turner Prize nominee in 1999. She represented the UK at the 2007 Venice Biennale and the same year she became a member of the Royal Academy of Arts. She also holds an Honorary Doctorate from the Royal College of Art, London; Doctor of Letters from the University of Kent, and Doctor of Philosophy from London Metropolitan University.

## BRYAN FERRY

Bryan Ferry began his musical career singing for a rock band whilst studying art at the University of Newcastle upon Tyne under Pop-Conceptualist Richard Hamilton. In 1970 he formed the glam-rock phenomenon Roxy Music. He has since gone on to carve out a successful music career both with Roxy Music and via his solo work. Bryan Ferry first met Isabella Blow in the early 1980s when she was living in New York. They began an incredibly close friendship which continued throughout her life. She was the godmother of his first child and was, in his own words, "part of his family."

## BOY GEORGE

English singer and songwriter Boy George became famous in the early 1980s with the pop group Culture Club. Well-known for his androgynous look, he became the poster figure for the New Romantic fashion movement in the UK. Culture Club disbanded in late 1986 and Boy George embarked on a solo career. He has also been a successful DJ since the early 1990s and in 2002 his musical *Taboo*, the story of his rise to fame featuring new songs and old Culture Club hits, premiered in London.

## JASMINE GUINNESS

Jasmine Guinness, of the famous Irish family, is a model, womenswear designer for www.very.co.uk, and co-founder of the charity Clothesline. She also runs a toyshop on Portobello Road in London's Notting Hill. A portrait of her by Mario Testino is held at the National Portrait Gallery in London.

## STEPHEN JONES

In the late 1970s Stephen Jones was a student at Central Saint Martins College of Art and Design, and by 1980 he had opened a millinery shop in London. His ambitious designs and radical materials soon began to draw fashionable crowds to his Covent Garden salon. Today, Jones continues to attract celebrities and royal clientele. He has collaborated with designers from Vivienne Westwood to John Galliano for Dior and his designs have regularly been seen on the runway. His work was shown at the V&A museum in the 2009 exhibition *Hats: an Anthology by Stephen Jones*.

## WOLFGANG JOOP

German fashion designer Wolfgang Joop began his career in fashion in 1970 when he and his wife won the top three prizes in a design competition. His fashion and cosmetics label Joop! was founded in 1981. He has since sold his shares in the company and in 2003 he launched his new label Wunderkind. He showed the first collection at New York Fashion Week in September 2004 and presented its first menswear collection during Milan Fashion Week and Paris Fashion Week in June 2009. He is also an illustrator and over one hundred of his works are on show at the Hamburger Museum für Kunst in Hamburg.

## DANIEL KLAJMIC

Photographer Daniel Klajmic was born in Rio de Janeiro in 1976. His work has been included in several international publications such as *Visionaire*, *The Sunday Times*, *V*, *Big*, and *i-D* magazine and his advertising jobs have included Max Factor and Pirelli. In 2004 he was honoured as a Hasselblad Master and he is also the youngest photographer to be part of the Pirelli collection at the Museum of Art of São Paulo. In addition to fashion and advertising he is also a documentary photographer and has exhibited his work in Rio de Janeiro and internationally. In 2006 he was part of the New Photographers Show in Cannes, curated by Getty Images.

## HILARY KNIGHT

American-based illustrator Hilary Knight was born in Hempstead, Long Island, and grew up in the town of Roslyn. When he was six his family moved to Manhattan, where he has stayed. He now has an apartment in the centre of New York City which doubles as his studio and houses his collection of books, programs, and recordings of theatre and film music. His first published work appeared in *Mademoiselle* magazine in 1952, and he followed it up with drawings in *House and Garden*, *Good Housekeeping* and *Gourmet* magazines. He has illustrated over fifty books, nine of which he also wrote, and continues to provide illustrations for many magazines.

## SHAUN LEANE

At the age of sixteen Shaun Leane started as an apprentice in London's jewellery quarter, Hatton Garden. He spent thirteen years in a traditional English workshop focusing on diamond mounting and antique restoration before embarking on a career in the fashion world. Twice awarded the UK Jewellery Designer of the Year title, Leane is internationally celebrated for pushing the boundaries of jewellery design and his work has been described by Sotheby's as "antiques of the future." Alongside his collections and bespoke pieces he designs for clients such as Sarah Jessica Parker and Daphne Guinness. His work with Alexander McQueen brought him international recognition.

## RUI LEONARDES

Fashion designer Rui Leonardes studied menswear and womenswear at the Gerrit Rietveld Academie in Amsterdam and went on to graduate with an MA in Fashion from the Royal College of Art in London. At the RCA he became famous for his shoe designs. He launched his collection of high heels for men at the MA graduate show in 2005.

## DONNA LOVEDAY

Donna Loveday is Head of Exhibitions at the Design Museum in London. She has extensive experience of curating high profile exhibitions of art, sculpture, photography and design at the Barbican Art Gallery, Royal Society of British Sculptors, British Film Institute and the Design Museum. At the Design Museum she manages an extensive exhibition programme and also leads an MA course for twenty-three students in collaboration with Kingston University, the first of its kind to link contemporary design with a career in the creative industry sector.

## ROXANNE LOWIT

Roxanne Lowit is a fashion photographer based in New York City. She has exhibited worldwide, including at the Metropolitan Museum of Art, the Whitney Museum of American Art and the V&A Museum in London. She has also produced photography for advertising and editorials. Lowit was one of the first photographers to take pictures backstage at fashion shows; she would encourage her model friends to sneak her in, and once she was there, she took photos that would give rise to the now popular backstage scene.

## MARIO TESTINO

Born in Lima, Peru, Mario Testino moved to London in the 1970s to pursue his interest in photography and is now one of the most well-known fashion photographers working today. He is famous for his editorial work for magazines such as *Vogue* and *Vanity Fair*, and he has also shot campaigns for fashion houses such as Burberry, Hugo Boss and Dolce & Gabbana. He has been shown in prestigious galleries and museums worldwide. In 2002 an exhibition of his work titled *Mario Testino: Portraits* was shown at the National Portrait Gallery in London.

## MARCUS TOMLINSON

London-based photographer and filmmaker Marcus Tomlinson's editorial work includes shoots for *The Face*, *Arena*, *Arena Homme Plus*, *Vogue* and *i-D*. He has also worked with Philip Treacy, Hussein Chalayan, Issey Miyake, Christian Lacroix and Hermès. Tomlinson has exhibited in art venues such as the Turbine Hall at Tate Modern, the Museum of Contemporary Art in Los Angeles, the Museum of Modern Art in Luxembourg and the Design Museum in Berlin. His films are often as suggestive as his photographs, frequently playing with appearance and disappearance, fragility and the ephemeral.

## PHILIP TREACY

The world's leading milliner, Philip Treacy was born in County Galway in Ireland and moved to London in 1988 to study fashion design at the Royal College of Art. In 1989 he took a hat to Michael Roberts, fashion director at *Tatler*, where he met Isabella for the first time. She asked him to make a series of hats for her wedding, launching his career. He won several British Designer of the Year awards, and many collaborative projects followed, including designs for Alexander McQueen's 1999 Haute Couture collection at Givenchy in Paris, and more recently for Grace Jones's Hurricane Tour in 2009, and for Lady Gaga in 2010. He has received an OBE (Order of the British Empire).

## ELLEN VON UNWERTH

Ellen von Unwerth is a German-born photographer and director. She worked as a fashion model for ten years before moving behind the camera herself, finding fame when she first photographed Claudia Schiffer for Guess? Jeans. She has been published in *Vogue*, *L'Uomo Vogue*, *Vanity Fair*, *The Face*, *Arena* and *i-D*, and has published several books of her work. In 1991 she scooped the first prize at the International Festival of Fashion Photography. She has since worked on major projects within the music industry, and has directed many music videos for high-profile clients.

## VALENTINO

Valentino (Valentino Clemente Ludovico Garavani) is a legendary Italian fashion designer famous for his eponymous label and longstanding career in the industry. He has designed dresses for celebrities ranging from Jacqueline Kennedy Onassis to Jennifer Lopez and is particularly famous for his wedding dresses. In 2006 he was awarded the Chevalier de la Légion d'honneur in France. He announced his retirement in 2007, and in the same year fellow international designers joined him in celebrations that took place over several days in Rome to honour his career. In 2008 the feature length documentary "Valentino: The Last Emperor" premiered at the Venice Film Festival.

## PRASHANT VERMA

Having trained at Alexander McQueen, Philip Treacy, John Galliano and Dior, fashion designer Prashant Verma has developed a body of work that attempts to go beyond fashion and looks for inspiration in history and philosophy. Following collections featuring flowing and colourful fabrics, Prashant's Autumn/Winter 2009 collection, *Meat*, took a tougher turn, featuring boxing championship belts, muscular fabrics and gladiatorial masks and shoulder pads.

## HARRIET VERNEY

Harriet Verney is the niece of Isabella Blow. She recently posed for influential photographer Nick Knight as part of the *SHOWstudio: Fashion Revolution* exhibition at Somerset House, for which Knight photographed one hundred of London's finest models, actors, musicians and artists. Isabella has been an inspiration to Harriet from the early days of her childhood.

## TIM NOBLE AND SUE WEBSTER

Tim Noble and Sue Webster are an artist couple who live and work together in East London. They met at Nottingham Trent University in the 1980s while studying on the BA Fine Art course. Their work has been included in shows worldwide and in the collection of Charles Saatchi. The couple often use found objects and rubbish in their work and use lights to play with shadows and to create powerful silhouettes. In 2008 they exhibited the work *Dark Stuff* at the British Museum. Composed of mummified animals the cat had dragged in, the work served as a dialogue with the ancient pieces in the museum's collection.

## LOUISE WILSON

Since 1992 Professor Louise Wilson has been the director of the MA Fashion Course at London's Central Saint Martins College of Art and Design, arguably the world's most influential and revered fashion college. Many of her former students have gone on to greatness, usually after taking part in the now legendary annual graduation fashion show held during London Fashion Week each year. The MA is the only fashion course in the world featured on style.com. She received an OBE (Order of the British Empire) for her services to education and the fashion industry in 2008.

## ANNA WINTOUR

Since 1988 Anna Wintour has famously held the post of editor-in-chief at American *Vogue*. Having decided to pursue a career in journalism at an early age, she took up a position at British *Vogue*, then returned to the US to work at *House & Garden*, before eventually going on to help revive *Vogue* in the US, to wide acclaim. In 2009 she became the focus of a critically celebrated film by R. J. Cutler, *The September Issue*. She has an OBE (Order of the British Empire).

# ACKNOWLEDGEMENTS

## MARTINA RINK

Thank you first to Isabella Blow, for being such a unique inspiration and for teaching me some fundamental things, like "always have a pen, paper and watch on you," and "red lips get you further in life."

My overwhelming thanks goes to all those who have taken the time to contribute to this book and to make it such a meaningful and insightful tribute to Isabella. A particular thanks also goes to Philip Treacy, Stefan Bartlett, Julia Delves Broughton, Lavinia Verney, and Lucy Birley, all of whom not only showed their support and faith in the project but helped to make it what it is.

Thank you also to the many people who were involved in putting the project together: Natasha Isaacs, Paul Sloman, Christine Antaya, Jamie Camplin and all at Thames & Hudson.

Many people also supported the book during its long journey. Thank you first to Dr. Norbert Rink and Ursula Rink and family, and also to Christoph Amend; Christiane Arp; Gayle Atkins and Lynette Cook; Cosima Bucarelli; Alice Bamford; Emanuel de Bayser; Regina Bellin; Natasha Binar; Detmar Blow; Marco Boito; Manuela Broderson-Horn and Felicitas Piegsda; Liza Campbell; Dihonn Carroll; Selcuk Cetinel; Sami Cohen; Nicholas Coleridge; Liana Daskalov; Freddy Dawes; Shelagh Delves Broughton; Kate Dewdney-Herbert; Ben Dodd; Stefan Eckert; Christine Eady; Leo Eberlin; Lisa Engelstädter; Sandrine and Angel Galbert; Peter Gray; Prof. Jo Groebel; Leah Halliday; Andrew Hansen; Reneé Lopez de Haro; Ana Finel Honigman; Helen Holden; Dr. Florian Landrebe; Joanna/MissLed; Jens Link; Daniel Lismore; Annalisa Maestri; Ernesto Montenovo; Kevin Maximilian Moran; Thorsten Moser; Jelka Music; Max Newman; Maria Neumann; Dr. Jens O'Brelle; Bomi Odufunade; Marcel Ostertag; Francesco Palombo; Niki Pauls; Tom Rebl; Patricia Riekel; Fiona de Rin; Angela Rusteberg; Michael Salac; Eva, Günther and Alexander Schulte; Marguerita Schumacher; Marcus Sell; Simon Settler; Rachna Shah; Nicolas Simoneau; Charlotte Smith; Desi Staneva; Joe Svenz; Dr. Gerd Teschke; Dawid Tomaszewski; Nina Tryon; Josef Voelk; Silke Wilhelm and Adam Wilkie.

The copyright of all photographs in the book remains with the photographers unless otherwise stated.